T0006951

Norma Dunning

AKIA
The Other Side

BookLand
press

Published by
BookLand Press Inc.
15 Allstate Parkway
Suite 600
Markham, Ontario L3R 5B4
www.booklandpress.com

Printed in Canada

Front cover image by Elvektorkita

Library and Archives Canada Cataloguing in Publication

Title: Akia: the other side / Norma Dunning.
Names: Dunning, Norma, author.
Description: Series statement: Modern Indigenous voices
Identifiers: Canadiana (print) 20220233160 | Canadiana (ebook) 20220233179 | ISBN 9781772311716 (softcover) | ISBN 9781772311723 (EPUB)
Subjects: LCGFT: Poetry.
Classification: LCC PS8607.U5539 A75 2022 | DDC C811/.6—dc23

We acknowledge the support of the Government of Canada through the Canada Book Fund and the support of the Ontario Arts Council, an agency of the Government of Ontario. We also acknowledge the support of the Canada Council for the Arts.

AKIA

The Other Side

This writing honours Inuit who lay in the past, and Inuit who are with us now and most importantly the Inuit who are waiting to come to us. Let us welcome them all with good hearts.

Table of Contents

Kishu's Brain

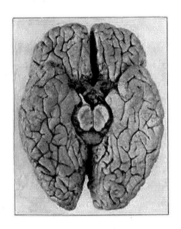

Whatever happened to Kishu's brain?
Is it still floating in formaldehyde
In a jar,
on a shelf,
layers and layers of dust
Wrapped around it like a lover's protective arms?
Who looks at it now?
Anyone?
Anymore?

The old black and white photo of he and his boy Menee
Arriving at Bellevue for medical care
Photographed standing side by side,
Father and Son
Naked.
Full frontal nudity.
disrobed and unveiled
At emergency unable to breath and spitting up blood

Inuit bodies do not include dignity

TB had slithered inside of their lungs
The only pest to arrive after the family's long trip with Robert

Bob? The Lieutenant?

Yeah, that guy.
The one who almost reached the north pole
On the backs of Inuit guides?
Yes him. The same guy who
Dipped himself inside of the little Eskimo girl
He photographed lying naked, across cold Arctic boulders

His obsession,
His pedophilia out on display
No one cared what a Whiteman stuck himself inside of
then even though she was less than 14 years-old

Inuit bodies do not include dignity.

Rob was a hero, an adventurer, an educated Whiteman
He brought Kishu and his family to join the Human Zoo

Look at those Eskimos,
putting on their furs and grabbing spears
Grunting and growling for the crowd who had come
to gaze inside their cages, confirming their suspicions that
Inuit are only animals

Inuit bodies do not include dignity

SubHuman
SubPar
Beastly feral cavemen
Not a family who were enticed by white money
And the prospect of having full bellies during a winter
Without blizzarding snow dotted with the icicles
Forming the hunger pangs inside a hollow gut

They went south after being baited and hooked
Into spending one winter on display
I wonder how much the zookeeper's bounty was worth?
To Catch and Keep
Not Catch and Release
A live Eskimo family?
The early beginnings of human trafficking for the sake
of science

Inuit bodies are without dignity

The report by Hrdlička titled, "An Eskimo Brain"[1]
Gives thanks to the originator of Kishu's autopsy
Gives thanks five years later
After bits and pieces
Of Kishu's body had been pickled
And preserved for almost 2,000 days and nights

Flesh floating inside of glass jars
An Eskimo saved for further slicing and dicing
By a scientist of infamy
The scalpel of his steady hand brings Kishu back to life

170 lbs, 1.64 m in height, muscular "and in every respect
normally developed" writes Aleš,
"Kishu was chief of his tribe."
Inuit never had 'chiefs'
Inuit had shared leadership
Consensus,
Aajiiqatigiinniq.

---

[1] *"An Eskimo Brain" found at: https://anthrosource.onlinelibrary.*
wiley.com/doi/pdf/10.1525/aa.1901.3.3.02a00050

Inuit ways are without dignity.

Kishu lived a life free of
A feathered bonnet,
his hair was never weaved into a singular braid
No tanned moose moccasins ever touched his toes
And yet in death he is declared a Chief of a tribe
A tribe of what?

Inuit tradition is smeared with Indian butter
Brown skins blend into beige
Ales writes, "Kishu was not racially distinct"
Indians and Eskimos are Siamese twins
Mirrored images of noble yet lowly savages

Hrlicka compares the brains of apes to that of Kishu
He makes reference to differences between
The grey matter of Whites and the Tanned Skins

Disappointment reigns in his findings
Eskimo brains, based on Kishu
Are on Par
Are Human
Developed and healthy

The scientist makes one stunned last plea:
"The marked differences of the specimens described…
in this paper from those of the whites, as well as among
themselves, makes a future acquisition of Eskimo
brains very desirable."

He coyly proposes an Eskimo culling
Inuit brains have become "very desirable"
He can not believe his own findings
Bring him more Inuit brains
Kishu is a fluke, a stroke of unlucky luck

Inuit bodies do have dignity.

Arctic Hysteria Pibloktoq

Bob's wife did this, wrote about
Inuit women as though they were dogs
Talked about the whores that her old man
Loved to lay with

She was white and knew her old man
The Commander
Was steppin' out on her
Rammin' his dink into dark-eyed women who liked 'it'

Liked to feel the strength of a man
Drilling and spinning and boring a deep hole of pleasure
inside of them
Liked the scent of his sweat mix with semen
Liked the taste of him and the way
His skin was damp after a long wrestle
That satisfied both of them

That is what Josephine saw,
Saw it inside of her head
On every night of each year
Because he never once reached out to her
Never once gave her pleasure or made her moan
Never once

An educated woman like her, married to a whoremonger
Married to a man who wanted to give himself
To dimwits, women without grace
Women who couldn't read or write
Or think beyond their tiny, perfect noses

She sailed with Bob
Took four long trips to watch him
Writhe inside of himself
His nervousness pleasured her
His strict politeness made her grin
Watching him perform like the perfect husband
A magnifying glass of obedience
Gave her the orgasm, she had longed for

She watched him watch those Eskimo women
Dirty bitches who laughed
too much
too long
Sneaking peaks at her then
smiling down at the tundra floor

She hated them
Hated their curious happiness
Hated how they always looked away
Never allowing a
reflection of her in their slanted dark eyes

Stupid women,
Trite Simpletons
Words of distaste
spilled and splattered
her journals each evening
Ink blots smearing their ignorance
Their imbecilic moments of hysteria
Running while peeling off their clothes
Women without shame

They called it Pibloktuq,
Arctic Hysteria
A running doltish display of the uncivilized
Who hid nothing,
No shame in nakedness
She watched with lustful longing
At their freedom to scream and strip off their clothes
Then fall to the ground, catatonic charades of
Hysteria unwrapping itself from white fox fur

The wife spoke to Bob and demanded
Restraint!
Tie her down! Straight-jacket that bitch!

The commander did as commanded
Wrapped her up in a sail from his ship
Tied and suspended her five feet off the ship's floor
A display of his deep devotion

The photo shows the white men
Lighting pipes with hot flames of giggles
Looking at the Arctic Mummy
Wrapped in her fear,
Loving their power over her body
Their power over her mind
Their white force of control
Suspending her body like a human swing

The Commander's wife writes a long essay
Puts it into print
How Inuit women are fools
How Inuit women are animals
In need of taming
In need of training
In need of colonial suppression,
Compression, Depression

Sipping her tea from a fine china cup
She sits years later
Smugly admiring the picture showing
Arctic Hysteria, Pibloktuq
Something a white jealous wife made up
To get back at the young adulteress
The Eskimo woman who took him away
From her bed
The power of white words from the wife of a Commander.
She got back at them all.

Author's note: Pibloktuq or Arctic Hysteria may now be what we call PTSD. Inuit women were raped and held as sex slaves to many early Arctic explorers. The north remains scattered with the remnants of their long ago sperm, Bob and all the early explorers begot so many babies but the women were never brought south, their children rarely recognized. Pibloktuq disappeared when the explorers headed back south.

What the Dickens is Wrong With Chuck?

The writer of classics, a wordsmith
A man driven by the insatiable need to knit words
Together, to string stories from his head
Onto the page

The plague of every writer

It is an illness.
The hours alone.
A solitary sickness.
Only the writer knows
How driven they each are.

Chuck knew it. He knew that he had
this one gift. The gift of words.

The words
that pulled him out of poverty and off the
dirty side streets loaded with back alley whores in the UK.
He was a rebel.
Loved to sit on the lips of the upper class
And shit down their ivory throats
His words about them were without respect
His words about them became Household Words

No longer were the wealthy
The only ones who received the printed page
He made sure that everyone had papers to read

The money in his pocket gathered steam
Jingling and Jangling all the way
To the next bottle of booze
The next cigar
The next whore
While his wife sat home with his ten progenies
There were so many of them
Chuck had not one clue what their names were

The affliction of the alcoholic
Names and faces become one large
Mess of tiny humanity who cry for food
And diaper changes
He had to flee to the comfort of the public houses
He had to maintain sexual hygiene
By fucking the whores who knew how not
To get knocked up

Sex is an oil change

He wrote and wrote and detested his wife
And all those damn kids but he
Wrote passed it all. Passed all the mayhem
That was his home life.
In time he had value. Success.
His elbows began to grease those of the rich.
He befriended them. Sought their company.
And they sought his.

Especially that one couple. The Franklins.
Jane and John.
They were travellers. Adventurers. She
was the monied one.
She was strong and tough and never wore
The band of slavery, a wedding ring

She was what every man longed to become

Coming out of retirement
For one last kick at the Can
John left town
Off he went to the Arctic
Off he went to the cold
Crusted ice without her

He never came back

Everyone waited and waited
Jane gathered up team after team to go find him
They returned empty handed
They returned without news
Without evidence
She was alone

Her hand embroidered silk Union Jack forever unfurled

Chuck saw his chance.
His chance to get on board
With a woman of power and prestige
He wrote
About the murderous Esquimaux
Heathens
Savages
He refused to believe Rae
The crew were not cannibals
Only the Esquimaux had
dined on kabobs of white men's knuckles
spearing flesh onto pointed tips
Appetizers from the Terror and Erebus

He wrote of Esquimaux cruelty
Wrote of Esquimaux greed
Wrote of Esquimaux anger
Wrote of the things that we never were

An ally to Jane
The Good Wife
Who lived out her days honouring John

Chuck, in all his drunkenness
In all his rage and fetish
For whores and 18-year-old girls
Inside of all his delirium tremors
He built a wall in his bedroom
To keep his wife away and
Printed words onto pages and pages
His own insanity was believed

Believed more than the Inuit
Who told countless explorers
That the Terror and Erebus
Are over there! Pointing to
Where the ships sank while
Retelling the stories of their ancestors

Chuck put his words into print
Inuit spoke their words into the memories
Of their children, the next generation

Chuck was believed

In September of 2014 HMS Erebus was found, two years later HMS Terror was found in Nunavut's Terror Bay, each in areas that Inuit had identified through Inuit Knowledge – the stories about the white explorers had been handed down for decades through Inuit Elders. It only took the world One Hundred and Sixty-Nine years to beleive us.

The Eskimo Identification Canada System

You knew about the E number system
The system you kept as a secret
But quietly wove into columns
On a page, a numeric ledger
Replacing humanity
To the bare bones of humility

When my baby was born
I was asked, "What's his name?"
I was proud to say "Hikhik"
I was given his ujamik instead
Told his name was Adam

I carried him,
I birthed him,
Saw his first breath
Heard his first cry
When no one was near I whispered
Hikhik into his left ear

The name of my attaatasiaq
A good hunter
A calm man
With gentle eyes and a voice as
Soft as sealskin

The man who gave me peace
Who served me comfort
Who kept me safe
Who called me irngutag

Grandpa left before Hikhik arrived
I had the next little one
I was proud to be tied to tradition
Honoured to not have Grandpa
Wandering the spirit-world without
An anchor

I raised Hikhik up
I taught him right from wrong
I gave him confidence
At school he was called E1-537
I resent that
I resent You

The man who said
"That the Eskimo will fall in line"
Spill out and spew the
Number that gives us food
Gives us breath, makes us less than human

You are a spider
A spider called Surreptitious
Who has weaved and spun and
Delicately created the
Lacey lies tied up in
The crooked cobwebs of colonialism

A snare trapping each of us
At different points while Surreptitious
Slyly grins and waits
Knowing the time will come

For truth
For reality
For certainty
To vomit from our guts

Blood vessels bursting
On the inside of ourselves
Waiting for Surreptitious
To pop the truth out of us

The man of military service
The man made of reports
And record books, whose biggest
Worry was whether or not to
Put a buffalo on the disc?

You and your men
Colonial Conspirators
In the clandestine life of Power
All I ever wanted was to
Have my boy carry the name
Of his Grandfather

A man of quiet dignity
My anger tires me
The web of expansion
A muddled soap opera
Explaining the lives of the controllers

They're proud and happy men
They made the Eskimo fall in line
They made us into numbers
Erased our smiles
Erased our faces
Erased our ancestors

They thought they were victors in
The battle that took place
On the empty tundra
Where one Inuit Elder
Dug into the ice afraid
of Jail Time because her necklaces were lost

Like all Inuit Moms
I took your tiny hand
One day and asked you to play
A remembering game

Told you that this was important
Not to us but to them
The whitemen who couldn't say
Our names and needed our help

Our language twists their tongues
And hurt their heads
So we said our numbers
To help them instead

Hikhik, you are smart
You learned with quick wit
I was pleased because you knew
The importance of your number

My son, my baby boy
Always honour your Grandfather
Always hold your head high
Hikhik, always remember

That Inuit are more than numbers

Stone Age Survivors

ESKIMO FAMILY. LIFE MAGAZINE.
FEBRUARY 27, 1956
Stone Age Survivors

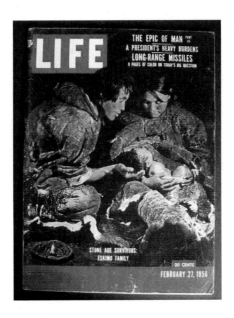

As defined by Merriam-Webster:
Stone Age: primitive, outmoded, or unsophisticated (as in ideas or
technology) by currently accepted standards

Words related to stone age: obsolescent discarded, disused, inoper-
able, unusable, unworkable, useless, dead, defunct, expired, extinct,
vanished

When I was a kid I loved Life
Loved the beautiful pictures
Loved to think that it was a magazine of importance
Loved thinking about how
If you were in Life – you had Life

One day I came upon this cover
The creche of the Inuit
Imellie and Joesphee
And their almost brand-new baby
I was appalled at Life

I was outraged at Life
Calling us 'Stone Age Survivors'
Backwards people, people without intelligence
People without Grace or Hope or Brilliance
In 1956

The year that John Diefenbaker took hold
The year that Elvis had one hit song after another
The year that a plane smashed into a Grey Nuns convent
And the Montreal Canadiens took their 8th Stanley Cup
Followed by the Edmonton Footballers 3rd Grey cup

While the rest of Canada jostled with
Their indulgence of sport and song
And bitched about Liberals and PC's
Ranting and raving and drinking
Pilsner Beer, swearing at refs and linesmen

Inuit were being used as Human Ammo
Lining us along the shores of the Hudson's Bay
Showing the Russians what sovereignty
Really looked like, Inuit were living
Proof of Canada's possession

Of the True North so very strong
So very free – free of food
Free of medical care
Free of proper education
Free of housing that kept bitter winds away
from our bodies

In 1956 Life took it upon themselves
To publish a Christmas Scene
Normally posted on a Yule card
And sent to family and friends
Life showed the world that we were still

Those of long ago
Those of dirty hair
Those without electricity
Those who still wore the skins
Of the animals they killed and ate

Life's cover padded the proof
Of White supremacy
White superiority
White advancement
Evolutionary progression

Life declares that Inuit
Are modern Mesolithic men
That we gorge on food today
And starve tomorrow
We are dated at 9600 BC in 1956

There are times when I completely hate Canada
Completely hate the lack of care
That is never extended to Inuit
Hate the way racism is kept quiet
While it dances in front of us day after day

Now years later
When I look at Life's cover
In 1956
I see the wonderment that
A newborn brings to his parents

I see the gentleness and beauty
Of a mother and father
And how their love is not
Something to be controlled
It is the wonderment of Life

It is the beauty of being Inuit
It is the open-expression of
Thankfulness, a reminder
Of what we should all be
Of how we should all see Inuit

People of perpetual tenderness
People of perpetual laughter
People of perpetual sharing
People of perpetual kindredness
Keepers of the Good Life

Edmonton Finally Drops the Eskimos

Edmonton's Canadian Football League franchise is the latest sports team to drop its racist name. THE CANADIAN PRESS/Darryl Dyck, July 2020.

It's a good day in Edmonton. It's a good day in Canada. It's a good day for Inuit.

After all the years that I and other Inuit Canadians have been complaining about the name of Edmonton's team in the Canadian Football League, it's good to know the franchise has finally decided it will no longer be known as the Eskimos.

It's been a long time coming, and it has finally arrived.

I've been an outspoken critic of Edmonton's refusal to rename its CFL team. As an Inuit writer and researcher, this has been a very personal cause for me.

My cause lies in the names of Joel, Isaac, Ellie, Mack and Aurora — my grandchildren, who I am hoping will never have to experience the E-word. They are brilliant and beautiful children who deserve to grow up in a world where racist terms won't harm them.

Years of campaigning

After years of campaigning for a name change, I wasn't confident the team would do the right thing.

One of Canada's top sports columnist said it would be "insane" to make the change now, given the costs associated with rebranding the team. I heard DJs on a local radio station lamenting that there wasn't a need for yet another sports team to change its name.

Through it all, I wondered why they never heard what Inuit were saying about a term we consider racist. As someone who has publicly criticized the team for years, I've been called the b-word and the c-word, among other things. To those people who filled my Facebook page with the most horrible language and the worst name calling, all I can say is shame on you again.

It's tragic to know that in 2020, there are still so very many people who will not hear the Indigenous side of an issue or who will sigh and say that they are sick of the constant change and everyone having a cause.

TRC head called for change

Sen. Murray Sinclair has been suggesting the need for a name change since he released the Calls to Action from his Truth and Reconciliation Commission in 2015. The commission listed several ways sports could lead to reconciliation, including the promotion of anti-racism awareness in sports. It only took five years for Edmonton to pay attention.

As an advocate for a name change, it's been disturbing that the general public doesn't understand the harm created by the E-word. They want to stay loyal to a team name instead of considering the opinions and feelings of the Inuit, the smallest Indigenous Canadian group that have the highest amounts of disparity.

Ignoring those feelings suggests it's OK that Inuit Canadians live their lives in poverty, that there remains food insecurity in the Canadian North based on the price of food alone and that most Inuit parents eat once a day so that their children can eat three times in a day. It's OK that teen suicide and drug and alcohol abuse is rampant and yet there are a lack of treatment centres in northern communities.

The word evokes stereotypes

The debate about the team name also revealed that most non-Indigenous Canadians don't want to examine their own racism. They don't want to think about what that E-word does to future generations of Inuit youth and small children. They don't want to think about what the E-word makes people think of — that cute little guy in a fur-ringed parka, standing next to a seal breathing hole with a harpoon in his hand.

Most of Canada doesn't want to think about how that E-word leaves Inuit Canadians in the time of long ago, as if we are not a progressive peoples who get out of bed and go to work as doctors and lawyers, nurses and teachers and who work towards a much better future for our children and the future generations that will come after us.

But now, at the end of a very long and sometimes hurtful campaign, I would like to thank the stakeholders and sponsors of the Edmonton team for their good conscience and acting on what they felt was right.

At the end of it all, all that matters to me is that Joel, Isaac, Ellie, Mack and Aurora will never have that word spoken to them. They are my heart. They drive my work, and I will always speak for them and all Inuit children. Ma'na. Thank you.

The E-Word

Social justice work
Is the most thankless and tiring work
Physical work is work that allows
Us to see that the end of our toil is near
Physical space and labour shows us such

Social justice work
Is the work of those who truly
Believe in creating a better world
Of making a future free of slander
Believing in fairness and righteousness
Is not an easy task

I feel embarrassment for the people
Who lost their shit over the name change
I feel sorry for the people
Who paraded their racism with public bravado
I felt shame for those who are without it

"Norma Dunning is a Zealot"
Publishes a southern Alberta newspaper
Perhaps I am a modern-day
Romans Resister
Or a fanatical fan of
Jewish theocracy

I am only a pursuer of fairness
Fairness being my religion
That I've touted inside of
The Bible of Morality
For seven years of Grey Cup finals

A national sportswriter spends column
After column writing of the innocence
Of the E-word, writes of the history of the team
And his investment
In team merchandise

His rage can't be tempered
He begins to write the word
Ex-Skimo inside of his column
I read all of his words and grin

White men really hate loosing

Edmonton's Historic Relationship With the Inuit

Edmonton's historic relationship with the Inuit is one of death, loneliness and despair. The Edmonton CFL team has finally changed its name after years of Inuit and non-Inuit supporters speaking out against its name. Before the team finally changed the name, they claimed in an online survey that the name was "originally chosen more than 100 years ago out of acknowledgement, perseverance, and hardiness of Inuit culture."

The team actually got its name from Calgary sportswriters in the 1890s who were mocking teams from Edmonton for how cold and northern their city was. Several sports teams in Edmonton then took up the name ironically. But I knew the story of a much different relationship between Edmonton and the Inuit. One of the strongest and most tragic connections between my people and the city of Edmonton is one of death, loneliness and despair all centred around the Charles Camsell Indian Hospital. Hundreds of Inuit came to the hospital in the '40s, '50s and '60s to be treated for tuberculosis. Many never returned home.

A city can change the name of their football team, but it can never change the history of lives lost and dismantled inside of a medical institution. On a recent walk in the area amid all the new construction that surrounds 128 Street and 115 Avenue, the old Camsell stands tall and stark. There have been several new windows placed into the aging structure but the redevelopment of the building into condos has been long delayed.

But when I stood there and looked at it again, I wondered how anyone could move into it. How could anyone think they could create a quiet life inside of a building that is loaded with the remnants of a medical genocide? Mixed with loneliness and heartache? How could anyone set up their lives in a building that was the site of so very many Inuit deaths. Inuit tears. Inuit loneliness. I stood there and thought, quviahunngittunga, I am sad.

I thought of all the Inuit who never returned home. Never saw their moms and dads smiles again. Never hugged a sister or brother again. Never stood in front of a husband or wife one more time. I think of the Inuit who were housed inside that hospital as Inuit who were without. Without love, comfort, and family. The elements that are required for real healing. I stood there and thought of how many Inuit spirits still wander through the Camsell hallways and who keep looking for those who loved them best. A spiritual searching and hoping for one familiar face. An eternity spent in limbo.

The official story is that when Inuit died at the Camsell they were buried in the St. Albert residential school graveyard. There is a cairn at the St. Albert public cemetery that remembers the 98 Inuit that are buried at the cemetery in unmarked graves. Thirty-one of those named on the cairn were children under the age of four. Some have their age marked as "baby," and who may have contracted tuberculosis from their mothers. Names on a plaque, a representation of the colonizer playing catch up.

For some reason, the government of the day thought it was impractical to set up sanitoriums in the north and to have Inuit heal at home. The colonial hand thinks it knows best as opposed to having Inuit in the care of their own, in their own communities filled with the love of family. In the eyes of our colonial past and present, we would never know what is best for us. How can we?

Inuit in Canada continue to contract tuberculosis at a rate of 290 times higher than all other Canadians. One of the reasons, according to a 2018 government of Canada report, is that "housing can be so crowded that residents sleep in shifts, as it is all too common for more than 20 residents to call a four bedroom house a home." For the population living south of sixty, the idea of living with 20 or more people under one roof is unthinkable. In the south we rarely even know who our neighbours are.

Inuit in Canada carry all the statistics that no one else wants. The highest rate of poverty, and food insecurity with many parents eating once a day so that their children can eat three times a day. The lowest levels of completing high school with a 35 per cent high school graduation rate in Nunavut. The saddest stat is that Inuit carry the highest rate of teen suicide. Future generations extinguishing themselves because they can not see a bright future.

Yet here in Edmonton the local football team had the audacity to say their team carried a moniker to honour the hardiness of Inuit while ignoring their true-life conditions. While the team spouted that public relations talking point the real connection between the city of Edmonton and the Inuit was a hospital that locked down hundreds of Inuit who never got home. The complete ignorance of the colonizer shines from the past into present-day.

Calvin Bruneau, the chief of the Papaschase band in Edmonton believes the southeast corner of the Camsell is a burial ground and contains unmarked graves of First Nations, Metis and Inuit children who died while in the care of the colonial medical system. Their names were never released into public record, and their bodies never returned home. Dub Architecture who is redeveloping the old hospital into condos has said that there is no evidence and have reassured the city of Edmonton that work will be halted, "if any bone is found" during the construction. Bruneau has asked for the province and the federal government to pay for an archeological dig to look for these remains. And before any further construction goes ahead, we need to know whether there are the remains of First Nations, Metis and Inuit children on the property.

Edmontonians should understand what Inuit went through inside the walls of the Camsell. Prime Minister Justin Trudeau issued an apology to the Inuit in 2019 for the mismanagement of the tuberculosis epidemic between the '40s and the '60s. He said, "We are sorry for forcing you from your families, for not showing you the respect and care you deserved. We are sorry for your pain. ...The racism and discrimination that Inuit faced, was, and always will be, unacceptable."

It is not okay that Inuit were rounded up like animals and placed onto ships that brought them south for treatment of an illness that they may or may not have had. It's not okay that the Charles Camsell Hospital received full federal payment for the long-term medical treatment of Inuit and that when that treatment was completed they were released onto Edmonton city streets with only the clothes on their backs and no airplane ticket to get them back home.

It is not okay that Inuit children and adults died and were buried here in unmarked graves, their bodies never returned to their loved ones. It's not okay that their loved ones were never told of their deaths or where they were buried because keeping track of dead Inuit bodies was simply not very important to Canadian authorities.

We get a sense of the loneliness and isolation that those Inuit at the Camsell must have felt now that we are living in the midst of the COVID-19 pandemic. People have experienced quarantine and the isolation that comes with it firsthand. Now imagine doing that thousands of kilometres from home in a totally alien environment you've never visited before, with your caregivers speaking a language that is foreign to you.

In happier moments I like to imagine a world free of colonialism. I like to imagine what it would have been like to have no interference in Inuit lives and to imagine what it would have been like to have Inuit arrive in Edmonton by choice, not by force. Let's build that world.

Aanniavik (Hospital)

The early morning that we strolled around him and I, I was heavy inside of my spirit. There was a strong sense of trepidation that laid inside of me. My heart felt like a 300-pound boulder.

He had never seen it before but he arrived researched and ready to walk. He saw a building under construction. I saw pain. He saw the remodelling of something old into something new. I heard screams and watched tears slide down the stucco.

Heavy equipment whirled around us like ballerinas. Swan Lake's cellos and violas played inside of my head. Mechanical earth movers bellowed past us. The stench of old mud and oil mixed into a storm of blurring brown. I didn't hear them. I heard the tempo rubato and I could not walk with an andante stride like he did.

I had walked here alone before. I was returning to a ground of grief. For me the return to this hollow building was an elegy to Inuit. He could not see what I felt.

Time is spent tearing down John A statues or throwing red paint onto his bronze and stone stature. We talk about decolonization and how to bring visibility to Indigenous Canadian history inside of a country that is not ready for it. Every city has buildings that contained Inuit in some form. Aanniavik, hospitals are supposed to be places of healing. Places of hope, of the return to good health and mind and spirit.

He looks over at me and asks what I think of the condos that are being created inside of a defunct building. He thinks the balconies look spectacular. I say that I can't imagine sitting on them. What I don't say is that I can imagine Inuit spirits looking out onto a city that treated them like refuse, human scraps of little boys and girls' bodies buried in the east garden waiting to go home and play.

He see progress. I see despair. We call this two different worldviews.

Non-Indigenous Intergenerational Ignorance

1. Denial

"Why did Canada lie to me?"
"Why didn't I hear this in school?"
My students always blubbering in front of me.

I never know what to do with them.
How do I comfort the lily-white offspring of colonialism?
Why would I want to?

Their shock and anger is bundled up inside
of pieces of tattered rage
Hanging off their bodies is The Maple Leaf
of Our Discontent
Some are insulted that an old Inuk Prof is The One

The One who broke their bubble of perfection
A protected space of never knowing
Of never having to deal with the reality of their homeland

Their homeland where inside their homes they were told
That our kind are all just drunks and druggies
Shitting out babies to get more welfare cash

Living the free life and being paid a monthly cheque
Because we're still breathing a tax-free existence
They end up in my university room, arriving smug

Smug and shiny and looking down their pristine noses
Confident that this old Inuk can't teach them
One damn thing that they don't already know

Confident that my PhD was handed over to me
Like candy on Halloween night
Profs Of Colour can't be as smart as the White Ones

The Hallowed Halls of Higher Learning
Are filled with Academics
Inside a black and white gumball machine

The machine that the students stick
Their fingers into, plucking out the coloured ones
Because those profs run popcorn classes

Candied popcorn coated in the blood of my Inuit ancestors
The ones who died while being shuffled around as
Human flagpoles of the true north

Strong and Free
Walk into my room thinking they know
Everything there is to know about Residential School

Until the bodies of Two Hundred and Fifteen children
Are found in BC
The little ones who never got to grow up at home

The little ones who never got to grow up at all
Students blubbering over a past
Their white guilt on display

Am I supposed to hug them and tell them
It will be alright?
We've been crying for over 150 years

It's their turn
It's their time
To make a reckoning

Their tears are too late to matter
A soliloquy of silence
Spreads across Canada, there is no balm in Gilead

2. *Anger*

All the slippery secrets of our country
Our country that sits as the best place in the world
To live in because we are so kind, so polite

"Would you like me to pull on your tongue?"
"Let's beat the little heathens!"
"Put them in their place!"

Words spoken to tiny children
Taken from Anaana and Ataata
The people who loved them best

For decades I heard it is not their problem
That it happened long ago and not one of their
family members hurt a brown kid

But they did
They hurt all the kids by not doing one damn thing
Standing in unity a Community of Complicit Canadians

Interfering would not be the Christian thing to do
Decades later the cries of little ones
Are heard from six feet under

And now they stand in front of me
Wanting me to wrap my arms around their remorse
Pat their white knuckles and say

"It'll be alright."
It will never be alright
Whites tally up their conspiracy theories - this is just

Just another money grab
Because that's all we do is expose painful pasts
To bump up our meagre bank accounts

Canada – you had it coming!
I'm so sick of all of you
So tired of your hate

3. Bargaining

The sins of the Father
Do fall upon the son
J.T. is cleaning up after P.E.T.

The son with his shit shovel
At the end of a century long
Parade of Death and Denial

Scooping it up and tossing it towards
The Pope, The Church, Anyone
But his own Backyard Archives

He tears up telling Canada that
It's hard to be a Catholic
As if he can relate

To what my Mom lived through
As if he understands
Her anguish floating in jugs of Kelowna Red

He absolves himself by saying
He'd asked for an apology
The last time he strolled into the Vatican

Listen to what he isn't saying
He doesn't speak of records in Ottawa
Watch him point across the ocean

The dollars begin to be offered
$27.1 million in total
Here's some cash, go find a dead kid!

The bargaining, the bartering
The sullen eyes of Canadians
Who refused to believe any of it

Government officials who publicly
Speak that they thought they were doing
Good and now even the UN can't stand to look at them

And the best place in the world to live in
Finally is seen as the imposter
It always has been, finally

4. Depression

Churches going up in flames
Red children hand prints
Splattered on Houses of God

I wonder how many white people
Are throwing red paint around
On all those venerated statues

Nellie and Winston and Frank
And the stain of their sins
Becomes public fodder

I wonder how many white people
Are lighting up churches
And falling in line with Christopher Hitchens

The crying of "I didn't know!
What can I do? Can I be your ally?"
Allies generally want personal gain

Advocates do not.
Educate yourself, read all the books
Take the time to inform your mind

Don't sit in my university classroom
With tears pouring down your face
And expect me to care, that you care

Because allies and activists are generally
Not in for the long haul
They're in for the here and now

And then everything returns to
Whatever normal is
We've all only ever wanted

The basics of life
The necessities of living
People who listen to our stories

People who believe in our words
And understandings People who care
To care forever, lighting a match doesn't cut it

5. *Acceptance*

Well Canada we've managed through
The Summer of Our Malcontent
We silenced Canada Day

Instead of pomp and showmanship
We had quiet reflection
And fireworks the little ones never saw

We had all the nationalists
And loyalists spouting off that their
Canada Day was being taken from them

And why should history be rewritten
To accommodate those Natives?
They are not the Founding Fathers

Of this country that keeps its lies under
Tight wraps of cellophane and unmarked graves
But let us remember the children

Let us remember how they are telling
Us their story now
Let us remember that their voices

Were left dormant for over one hundred years
An Abyss of Abeyance
A void that is now being filled

Let us remember their mothers and fathers
Who spent a life time looking out the window
In hopes of seeing them walking the path to home

Let us remember their aunties and uncles
Who wanted them back to teach
Them how to be good people

Let us remember their brothers and sisters
Who never got to play tag or
Hide and Go Seek with them

The children are talking to us now
Let us remember compassion and care
Let us remember the love

They never got to give to all
Those who love them still
Let us take this time Canada

Because those little ones will
Keep talking until thousands of
Small voices are heard

It's time for Canada to accept
It's truth
It's time for Canada to

Reconcile its records
It's time for Canada
To hear the voices

Of the small ones
And admit its genocide
It's time for Canada

To come clean
And
Step up and maybe we can all 'Just get over it.'

Authors' note:

This poem was written before the 2022 Papal Visit by Pope Francis. It is my hope that his validation of the suffering of Indigenous Canadians from past policies   and their continued effect on present day Indigenous lives is remembered and that his apology has initiated healing.

Future We In-u-Wee

Are we allowed to dream?
Are we allowed to exceed the parameters of a reality
   that Canada has no interest in?
Are we allowed to be more and better and complete?

Aren't we all supposed to stay in the time of long ago?
The time of standing at a seal breathing hole with
   a harpoon pointing towards small shivers of ice water.
A time of long patience and short lives.
A time of used-to-be.

Used-to-be that Inuit knew their place.
Used-to-be that Inuit only stayed north of sixty
   and not south.
Used-to-be that Inuit never spoke unless there was
   a camera in front of them.
Used-to-be that Inuit kept their faces out of media
   unless they were dead or dying.
Used-to-be that Inuit could go hungry and no one
   had to deal with it.
Used-to-be that Inuit were used to being.

Used to being the people thought of as cute and cuddly.
Used to being the people who were savagely sexy.
Fuck a skimo and white is not alright.
Used to being the White Ones doormat.
Used to being the place where all the excrement of
    whiteness laid their visceral leftovers.
Puddles of sperm.
Puddles of snot.

Used to being human spittoons.
Used to being a disk number and not a name.
Used to being moved around,
Bedouins of the Hudson Bay shoreline
Used to being human flag poles.

Used to being Canada's biggest afterthought.
An afterthought of every government riddled
    with Alzheimer's.
An afterthought named The Forgotten Ones.

The Forgotten Ones who can still go hungry in 2022.
The Forgotten Ones with twenty-two people crowded into
one house. Do not move or you lose your sleeping spot.
The sleeping spot you marked with the stench of you.

The Forgotten Ones are made even more forgettable
    if they dare to move south of sixty.
The land claims made sure of one thing; the thing called
    Don't You Dare.

Don't You Dare try to make a better life for yourself.
Don't You Dare think that your kids deserve a chance.

A chance at a better education.
A chance at being someone. Someone with a university
degree. Someone who practices law or nursing or teaching
outside of the invisible borders that confine us into a
tight little cluster of long ago.

Don't You Dare dream of a future.
Don't You Dare dream that you have somewhere
  to go when there is no where to go.
Don't You Dare dream that once you are south that
  people will look at you as one of them. You're a freak.

A freak on a city sidewalk, panhandling his life away.
A freak who cannot talk without that accent, anyways eh.
A freak in the limbo of north and south.

South is purgatory.
South is where you get asked if all your kids have the
  same dad.
South is where you cannot apply into northern
  scholarships.
South is where you get asked if you are Spanish.
South is where you are not really Inuit if you are not
  eating raw meat.
South is where speaking Inuktitut makes you real.
South is where you are asked if you can speak Cantonese.
South is where you get to disappoint people twice in
  under sixty seconds.

South is where your Inuk head glaringly sits on
StatsCan charts.
South is where StatsCan graphs shows you finished
high school.
South is where StatsCan graphs will make you look like
a success.
South is where you get a job because you are Inuk.
South is where university degrees tucked inside your
back pocket do not count.
South is where you get hired because a boss has to fill
her Indigenous quota.

South is where you get used for your community
contacts.
South is where white people harvest your Inherent
Knowledge.
South is where exploitation of who and what you are
happens.
South is where the northern Inuit look down their
small noses at you.
South is where you are neither home nor away
South is where you become a non-Nunangat Inuk

A new title.
A new you.
A new anyone else.

If we could live in a world without borders
We would not be different from one another
What if in the future we were not points on a compass
What if the north pole de-magnetized

Allowing all Inuit to de-tox
their thoughts
De-liberately
De-ciding to
De-vote themselves
To one another

What if Inuit stopped letting invisible lines
De-Vide Us
Lines that we can not see or touch or smell.

What if Future We In-u-wee fell into each other,
What if Future We In-u-wee were people without gravity

Nose-diving into love with one another
Twisting and twirling and twitching
Flooding ourselves in the rapture of angelic care
Towards one another

What if Inuit Nunangat, our homeland was here
    and every where?

And Future We In-u-wee recognized each other
As the Family of The People
No matter where we stand
We are not the remnants of long ago

We are here
We are now
We are the shadows of each other
Wrapped in the cocoon of Creator's hand

A cocoon spun with the fondness of our future selves.

Future We In-U-Wee have food that make their
  bellies burst
Future We In-U-Wee have homes with bedrooms
  for everyone
Future We In-U-Wee have diplomas and degrees
  dangling from their walls
Future We In-U-Wee do not court difference

Future We In-U-Wee
Is today not tomorrow
Future We In-U-Wee
Is the us we are supposed to be

Let us Inuit hold hands
Let us Inuit skip together
Into Future We In-U-Wee

I wrote this piece out of the love and hate and disappointment and pride that I have in who Inuit are. I wrote this piece out of the racism that I have experienced as an Inuk scholar living in the south. I wrote this piece because I know what it is like to have governments ignore hunger. Ignore crowded housing. Ignore tuberculosis, a disease absent in the southern areas of Canada but rampant in the north. Ignore Inuit children who are not completing high school. We truly are Canada's biggest afterthought.

I wrote this piece because of the rejection I feel from my own. Lateral violence sneaks into our Inuit consciousness and lays there waiting to pounce on one another. I hate that we buy into colonial measures and markers of each other. Our ancestors did not do that. Our ancestors welcomed everyone and gave love as their first ingredient to each of us. We have forgotten that.

When I wrote the word, "In-U-Wee" I was thinking of how often the word "Inuit" falls out of non-Inuit mouths in the form of "In-You-It" or "In-O-Wheat" and an assortment of other barnyard sounds. Our own absence as a people in Canada is never articulated properly. As I continued writing "In-U-Wee" it became a word of fun and hope and I could hear that 'Wee' echoing inside of my head.

I thought of when my sons were small ones and I would grab their wrists swing them into the air and say, "Wee Wee Wee" and they'd laugh as their bodies wrote waves splashing into the air. Saying the word 'In-U-Wee' sounded like riding on a rollercoaster and the fun and excitement and the unknown positive possibilities that lay inside of Inuit future generations. Future fun. Future success. Future us.

Our future is now, not tomorrow. Our future is here. Our future lies within our next breath.

Glossary

Attaatasiaq – Grandfather

Aanniavik – Hospital

Irngutag – Grandchild

Ujamik – Necklace